When Winter Comes!
A Kid's Guide To Lillehammer, Norway

Photography by John D. Weigand
Poetry by Penelope Dyan

Bellissima Publishing, LLC
Jamul, California
www.bellissimapublishing.com

Copyright © 2017 by Penny D. Weigand and John D. Weigand

All rights reserved. No part of this book may be reproduced or transmitted in any form or by any means, electronic or mechanical, including photocopying, recording, or by any other means, or by any information or storage retrieval system, without permission from the publisher.

ISBN 978-1-61477-275-0
First Edition

"It's not what you look at that matters, it's what you see."

Henry David Thoreau

When Winter Comes!
Bellissima Publishing, LLC

Introduction

At the city centre of quaint Lillehammer you will find late 19th-century wooden houses that overlook the northern part of lake Mjøsa and the river Lågen. The town is surrounded by high, beautiful mountains, which is why this city hosted the 1994 Winter Olympics and the 2016 Winter Youth Olympics. There is a very old saying in Norway that if you are a true Norwegian, you were born with skis on your feet. This may be true, because the Norwegian people have been skiing for over 4000 years! Norwegians also believe there is no such thing as bad weather, only bad clothes; and they love to go on tour! When they meet others who are on tour, they greet them with the words, "God tur," which means, "Have a good trip!"

So "God tur," and have a good trip as you travel vicariously through the pages of this "learn to read" book created just for kids by the award winning author, attorney and former teacher, Penelope Dyan, and photographer, John D. Weigand, and see a bit of what they saw when they visited this 1994 Winter Olympics host city. When you are done, watch the free music video that goes with this book on Bellissimavideo's YouTube channel. And remember. . . when learning is fun, kids love to learn!

When Winter Comes!
Bellissima Publishing, LLC

When Winter Comes!
A Kid's Guide To Lillehammer, Norway

Photography by John D. Weigand
Poetry by Penelope Dyan

You hop on the train at Oslo;
and you wonder,
"What will I see?"
You rub the arms of your jacket.
You're as cold as you can be!

You arrive in Lillehammer.
Past an empty park you walk.
Your mom and dad talk and talk.
Then they look at you; and Mom says,
"My dear,
this is Lillehammer.
Did you know that the 1994
Winter Olympics were held
right here?"

You see a church, and your parents
are even more excited than before;
but then. . .
YOU weren't even BORN in 1994!
You wonder and you think,
"What else is there to see and do?"
As if reading your mind, Mom says,
"You'll see a lot MORE,
before WE are through!"

The town's centre is VERY colorful,
as YOU can clearly see.
Mom says,
"This is such a lovely place to be!"

For a moment, you all stop,
where a bicycle sits in front of a shop.
Dad adjusts his backpack,
Mom fixes her hair,
and in the next window you stop
and you ALL stare.

And what is it that you see?
You see a lovely tea service.
It's all set for tea!

Next you see. . .
right in front of your two feet,
three purplish pink pots of pansies
on the sidewalk by the street!

And then you see,
right out of the blue,
two colorful stuffed owls staring
right at you!

You see a kid dressed in blue
(wearing a pink hat)
staring at some pansies
in a VERY great BIG pot!
And THAT kid looks good and hard;
And THAT kid looks a lot,
right down at those purple pansies
in that VERY great BIG pot,
as if studying by EVERY single minute,
and EVERY single hour,
EVERY single petal
of EVERY single flower!

Then you see a kid wearing
some old comfortable boots of brown,
walking on those new cobblestones,
placed right there on the ground!

Then as back toward the park,
you and Mom and Dad wend,
you realize that another adventure
is coming to its end,
You stare upon what looks like
a pond of snowy ice,
and you think about how staying warm
is oh so VERY nice.
And then you think
(as every TRUE Norwegian knows)
there really is NO such thing
as bad weather,
when you are wearing
nice WARM clothes!

You get back to Oslo; and Mom asks,
"Did you see with your eyes,
or did you see with your heart?"
And you both agree
it's with the heart, learning starts.
And you also both agree
there is ONE truth from which
no one CAN hide,
when it comes right down to it,
we are ALL the same inside. . .
except that it is said that Norwegians
are born with skis on their feet!
AND because this is a cold, cold place,
you BOTH think THAT is neat!

"Sometimes walking away is a step forward."

Author Unknown

"Or maybe you can ski away!"

Penelope Dyan

www.ingramcontent.com/pod-product-compliance
Ingram Content Group UK Ltd.
Pitfield, Milton Keynes, MK11 3LW, UK
UKHW060135240426
12048UKWH00002B/52